A World of Field Trips

Going to a Museum

Rebecca Rissman

Heinemann Library
Chicago, Illinois

www.capstonepub.com
Visit our website to find out more information about Heinemann-Raintree books.

To order:
☎ Phone 888-454-2279
▭ Visit www.capstonepub.com
to browse our catalog and order online.

Edited by Rebecca Rissman, Dan Nunn, and Catherine Veitch
Designed by Richard Parker
Picture research by Tracy Cummins
Originated by Capstone Global Library Ltd
Printed and bound in China by Leo Paper Products Ltd

15 14 13 12 11
10 9 8 7 6 5 4 3 2 1
0426

Library of Congress Cataloging-in-Publication Data
Rissman, Rebecca.
  Going to a museum / Rebecca Rissman.
    p. cm.—(A world of field trips)
  Includes bibliographical references and index.
  ISBN 978-1-4329-6067-4 (hb)—ISBN 978-1-4329-6076-6 (pb)
1. School field trips—Juvenile literature. 2. Museums—Juvenile literature. I. Title.
  LB1047.R575 2012
  371.3'8—dc22   2011015151

Acknowledgments
We would like to thank the following for permission to reproduce photographs: Alamy p. 9 (© Richard Green); Corbis pp. 4 (© Image Source), 12 (© Atlantide Phototravel), 14 (© C3Image Source), 20 (© Pascal Deloche/Godong), 22 (© ANDY RAIN/ epa); Getty Images pp. 11 (Stephen Chernin), 13 (JANEK SKARZYNSKI/AFP), 15 (China Photos), 18 (Alex Wong), 23b (China Photos); Photolibrary pp. 7,8 (Robert Ginn/Index Stock Imagery), 17 (Diaphor La Phototheque), 19 (Russell Gordon), 21 (Pawel Libera), 23a (Robert Ginn/Index Stock Imagery), 23d (Diaphor La Phototheque); Shutterstock pp. 5 (© Vaclav Volrab), 6 (© Jorg Hackemann), 10 (© Brykaylo Yuriy), 16 (© Matthew Jacques), 23c (© Jorg Hackemann).

Front cover photograph of children at the Natural History Museum, London reproduced with permission of Glow Images (Norbert Michalke). Back cover photograph of a history museum reproduced with permission of Shutterstock (© Brykaylo Yuriy).

Every effort has been made to contact copyright holders of any material reproduced in this book. Any omissions will be rectified in subsequent printings if notice is given to the publisher.

Contents

Field Trips

People take field trips to visit new places.

People take field trips to learn new things.

Field Trip to a Museum

Some people take field trips
to museums.

Museums are places where special things are kept.

Museums display things in exhibits.

Some exhibits change often.

Other exhibits stay the same.

Different Museums

This is a history museum.

It helps us learn what life was like a long time ago.

This is a science museum.

It helps us learn about how
things work.

This is a natural history museum.

fossil

It has fossils of animals that lived long ago.

This is an art museum.

sculpture

It has sculptures, paintings,
and drawings.

This is a space museum.

planet

You can see planets on
a large screen.

How Should You Act at a Museum?

Remember to stay with your group.

Only touch things if you are told it
is okay.

What Do You Think?

What kind of museum is this?

Look on page 24 for the answer.

Picture Glossary

exhibit collection of special things on display

fossil remains of a plant or animal that have turned into rock

museum place where special things are kept and shown. There are many types of museums.

sculpture type of art that an artist carves, or makes out of a material such as stone, wood, or clay

Index

Notes to Parents and Teachers

Before reading
Explain to children that a field trip is a short visit to a new place, and that it often takes place during a school day. Ask children if they have ever taken a field trip. Tell children that museums are places where special objects are kept. People go to museums to learn, see new things, and have fun! Ask children if they have ever been to a museum. If so, ask what type of museum it was and what they saw there.

After reading
- Write Dinosaurs, Art, Space Shuttles, and Costumes on the board. Then ask children what type of museum they should visit to see each object.
- Ask children to make a list of rules for how to behave when visiting a museum. Include staying with the group and being polite. Write their answers on a poster and hang it in the room.

Answer to page 22
It is a science museum.

NOV. 2012